WAYS

OF

WRITING

A GUIDE TO COLLEGE COMPOSITION

THIRD EDITION

THE WRITING CENTER
at PORTLAND STATE UNIVERSITY

The idea for this book grew out of conversations with Freshman Inquiry
faculty in 2007—particularly Joel Bettridge and Ann Marie Fallon. The
content of the first and second editions was written by PSU Writing Center
staff: Daneen Bergland, Kyle Cassidy, Benjamin Craig, Kenneth Crockett,
Dan DeWeese, Matthew Gallaher, Jodi Geren, Matthew Hein, Matt Kincaid,
Sarah Kruse, Shawna Lipton, Alexis Nelson, Josh Patrick, Grier Phillips,
Jonathan Sturgeon, Rachel Tobie, and Keri Thomas. Revisions and additions
in the third edition were written by Jacqueline Alnes, Lucas Bernhardt,
Wendy Bourgeois, Benjamin Craig, Alex Dannemiller, Dan DeWeese, Sarah
DeYoreo, Sarah Huddleston, Alissa Nielsen, and Thomas Van Camp. The
PSU Writing Center would like to thank Annie Knepler of University Studies
for her feedback, and Susan Kirtley and Hildy Miller for their continued
guidance and mentoring regarding strategies for teaching writing.

Original book design by Rachel Tobie.
Second edition designed by Lauren Shapiro.
Minor alterations for third edition made by Dan DeWeese.
Cover of this edition designed by Benjamin Craig

ISBN-13 978-0-9825101-1-7

Printed in the United States of America

Contents | ALPHABETICAL

Contents | CATEGORICAL

How do I get started?

How do I use sources?

Contents | CATEGORICAL

How can I make it better?

How can others help me?

INTRODUCTION

WRITING AS A PROCESS

Many writers suffer at the mercy of the great myth of "getting it right the first time." This myth tells us that the best way to write is all at once. Ideally (according to this myth), a writer opens a new computer document, composes an introduction, and then begins to type one paragraph after the next in an orderly fashion until, upon reaching the length requirement, the writer composes a nice conclusion that ties everything together, hits print, and is done.

This rarely happens. Our thoughts do not often spontaneously spool out in well-stated grammatical sentences arranged in a logical and effective order. The mind associates freely: a thought about computers leads to a thought about a music playlist on your computer, which leads to a thought about a concert, which leads to a thought about money, which leads to a thought about things you don't have, which leads to a thought, strangely, about moon rocks. Or something like that.

Thought may proceed this way, but an essay cannot. So writers often find themselves in a deadlock with that heartless little cursor, struggling to type the next line while believing that what they are writing lacks direction. It seems unavoidable, this confusion and uncertainty, especially if you feel that every word is set in stone. If you feel every written word is permanent, it makes sense to pause before writing the next word. And before the next sentence. And, again, before the next paragraph. It becomes dangerously easy, in that frame of mind, to become permanently paused.

But fear not. There is hope.

The next time you begin a writing project, try thinking about it as a series of steps that you can start and stop several times, as opposed to completing all of them at once. Knowing that you're going to let yourself go back and fix things later will keep you from having that "every word I write is set in stone" feeling, and most people write much faster and produce better material when they give themselves the freedom to write a first draft with a few rough edges.

A writing project that includes a drafting process—some pre-writing brainstorming, the composition of a draft, some reorganization and fixing, and strategies for straightening things up when you're done—will usually help you write faster, make your writing time feel more productive, and strengthen the quality of your final product.

This book is intended to suggest ideas and strategies that are helpful throughout the process of writing. It's also meant to be practical: short, easy to read, and full of "how to's" for completing class assignments, or for any time you have to write something.

Keep in mind that most writing strategies can be used in multiple ways and at different stages in your process. You might use some of the techniques in the "Generating Ideas" entry when you're just getting started on a paper, for instance, and then you might use them again when you've finished a draft and need to come up with new ideas for a revision.

Likewise, though you should obviously bring this book to the class in which it was assigned, we've tried to make the information within it practical for any class you have that requires writing. Our goal is that this book will be helpful to you not just this year, but in your future writing projects as well.

ACTIVE READING

Professors love to assign reading—hundreds of pages of the stuff! And they expect you to do more than just *read* all of those words—you have to *think* and *have ideas* about them. *Have class discussions. Write long papers.* It can be exasperating.

A good way to keep track of all that reading is by using a reading journal to write questions about things you don't understand, and to paraphrase the material you think is most important. You can underline key passages, circle points you have a comment or question about, use colored highlighters, or even put "?" or "!" in the margin so you can easily find particular passages later. Some people call this "annotation"— it's a kind of intellectual graffiti.

After you're finished annotating the text, you might:

> • Paraphrase the key passages—try to write them in your own words.

> • Write comments about circled passages.

• Write out any questions you have about circled passages, and then try writing answers. You don't need to know the answers—your thoughts on what they might be will be useful for a paper or a class discussion.

• Spend five or ten minutes freewriting about what you read. Begin with something that interests you from your notes, and write out any and all thoughts or connections you can think of.

• Read through your journal when you're finished, and do some active reading on *yourself* by underlining your best thoughts or points to develop further.

Presto! You have notes on the text and your responses to it. You'll have smart stuff to say in class, and when it comes time to write your next paper, much of the preliminary work of looking back over the reading will already be done. You'll be ready to get writing.

PRACTICE: During your next reading assignment, do one or all of the suggestions from this chapter: paraphrase, comment, question, and freewrite.

AUDIENCE

All writers make decisions about what written voice is appropriate for a particular piece of writing. Rather than making an abstract decision about what constitutes a "correct voice," consider the intended audience, then write accordingly.

For instance, if you were to write an email to a friend about a movie you'd recently seen, the writing could sound like:

> So like a million people, I went and saw *Night of the KilBot* last weekend. The alien robots were awesome!!! But the acting was ridiculous, and there's no way Scarlett Johansson could conquer a Bone-Krushing KilBot using only a re-wired cell phone. Whatever!

This voice is perfectly appropriate for a casual email to a friend, and the opinions are clear. If you were writing those same thoughts for a newspaper, though, your sense of a wider reading audience would shift the voice to something like:

> The computer-generated robots were first rate, but the dialogue left something to be desired.

When you're writing a formal paper in a university setting, the written voice shifts again. Your immediate reader will obviously be your instructor, but references to a specific reader in a personal or casual voice (i.e., "I don't know if you know what the KilBots did next, Prof. Smith, but it was so awesome that the scientific community could only say, 'Oh, snap!'") sound odd and aren't appropriate. This is because the assumed audience for college writing isn't a single person, but a larger body of educated readers—people who know enough about your topic to grasp your thesis and evidence. The written voice that results from assuming this audience is often called "academic voice."

A university paper about a film, then, might be expected to include discussion of visual composition, use of terms like "mise-en-scène," or (in this example) thoughtful analysis of artificial intelligence. The voice might sound something like:

> The robots' search for acceptance on an unfamiliar planet creates a sense of pathos in the viewer, though the surprising complexity of the androids greatly contrasts with the flat performances of the human players.

Writing for an academic audience might require some extra attention at first, and small adjustments might need to be made based on what field you're writing about. (Some fields are okay with the use of "I" in a formal paper, for instance, but others aren't.) In time, however, writing in an appropriate academic voice becomes more natural, and an ability to analyze what's appropriate for your audience can often help you decide how to phrase thoughts clearly and effectively in any piece of writing.

PRACTICE: Look at an important paragraph in the current draft of a paper you're working on. If you were to rewrite that paragraph for a radically different audience, how would it sound? How would you rewrite it for a third audience?

CITATION FORMATS

Two major systems for formatting and citing sources in a paper are used in undergraduate courses: MLA (Modern Language Association) and APA (American Psychological Association). Individual departments or disciplines may use even other citation styles, but MLA and APA are the most common.

The organizations responsible for creating these systems publish style guides to help writers understand and use them. These style guides describe how your paper should be formatted and how you should cite the ideas of others within your writing. The three major areas covered by each style guide include:

> • *In-text citations*: How to signal to your reader that you are making use of ideas that come from your reading or other outside sources.

> • *End citations*: How to list all of the sources you used to write your paper.

> • *Formatting*: How to set up margins, spacing, and titles, which font and font size to choose, what your first page should look like, and other similar details.

Citations are essentially notes that help readers track down original sources, and every field uses the citation style that best suits its interests and values. English majors use MLA because MLA citations include page numbers, and if an English major (or professor) wanted to find a quote a writer used, the page number is the information that is most important. Sociology majors use APA because that style includes the publication date instead of the page number, and it's more important in sociology to know what year quoted information was originally written. Since undergraduate students take courses in varying disciplines, the citation format you use will depend on your instructor's preference.

Clearly citing sources will lend you credibility by showing that you consulted other experts and have given credit to those who first developed specific ideas or published certain information. Using someone else's ideas or information without citing their source is considered plagiarism, a serious offense in a university course. It is important to note that you do not only cite sources that are quoted in your work. You should cite any time you use an idea that came from a source, whether that idea appears in your paper as a quote, paraphrase, or summary. (For more on these three tools for incorporating the ideas of others, see p. 46 of this book.)

Here are what citations look like in the body of a paper:

MLA Format: In *The Life of Addison,* Johnson further acknowledges the biographer's difficulties: "What is known can seldom be immediately told, and when it might be told it is no longer known" (116).

or

In *The Life of Addison,* the biographer's difficulties are further noted: "What is known can seldom be immediately told, and when it might be told it is no longer known" (Johnson 116).

APA Format: Bloom (2009) tells us that because it is clear and concise, the bill has made the "organic" classification "much easier for farmers and food distributors to understand" (Bloom, 2009).

Once you know which style your instructor wants you to use, it's easy to find places to look to make sure you are citing your sources clearly. Three resources are:

• *Writing Handbook or Style Manual:* Most good writing handbooks have basic information on MLA, APA, and Chicago formats. For more information, each of those organizations puts out their own, highly detailed book about their citation system.

• *Online Resources:* There is a wealth of citation help online, including the resources section of the PSU Writing Center's website (www.writingcenter.pdx.edu).

• *Writing Center:* Staff at the Writing Center are happy to help you find resources on any citation style.

Anatomy of an MLA End Citation

A paper in MLA style will include a list of sources at the end of the paper called a "Works Cited" page. In order to complete the citations for this page, you will need to gather information about your sources. A typical entry might include an article from an academic journal. To cite an academic article you will need to gather the following:

Author Name – The published name of the author or authors of the article
Article Title – The full name of the article as published
Journal Title – The full name of the journal
Year of Publication – The year of the original publication of the issue in which the article appears

Volume Number – Frequently appears on the cover or title page of the journal
Issue Number — Frequently appears on the cover or title page of the journal
Medium of Publication – Print or Web

The general format for an MLA end citation, then, is:

Author Last name, Author First name Author initial. "Article Title." *Journal Title* Volume number. Issue Number (Year of Publication): page number–page number.

Note: Sources published on the Internet also require the date you accessed the source online. The above list is only meant as a guideline of basic information. Many types of sources will require additional or different information. For a more exhaustive list of variations, see the *MLA Style Guide*. (For an example of an MLA works cited page, see page 93 of this book.)

An example:

Applegate, Brandon K. "Of Race, Prison, and Perception: Seeking to Account for Racially Divergent Views on the Relative Severity of Sanctions." *American Journal of Criminal Justice* 39.1 (2014): 59-76. Print.

Note that in the example citation, the first line of the citation is aligned to the left side of the page and the following lines are indented. This is called a "hanging indent." You may need to consult a resource to learn how to do a hanging indent on your word processing software.

Anatomy of an APA End Citation

An APA formatted paper will include a list of sources at the end of the paper titled "References." In order to complete the citations for the References page you will need to gather information about your sources. A typical entry might include an article from an academic journal. To cite an academic article you will need to gather the following:

Author(s) and/or Editor(s) Name – The published name of the author or authors of the article and/or the editor or editors
Publication Date – Year of publication
Article Title – The full name of the article as published
Journal Title – The full name of the journal
Volume Number – Frequently appears on the cover or title page of the journal
Issue Number – Frequently appears on the cover or title page of the journal
URL – The full web address, if using an Internet source

The general format for an APA end citation, then, is:

Author/Editor Last Name, Author/Editor First Initial. Author/
     Editor Middle Initial. (Publication Date). Article Title.
     Journal Title, Journal Volume(Journal Issue), page
     number—page number.

Note: This example is one simple variation. For details on any sources that don't fit the above, consult the *APA Style Guide*.

An example:

Applegate, B. K. (2014). Of race, prison, and perception:
     Seeking to account for racially divergent views on the
     relative severity of sanctions. *American Journal of
     Criminal Justice, 39*(1), 59-76.

Note that in the example citation, the first line of the citation is aligned to the left side of the page and the following lines are indented. This is called a "hanging indent." You may need to consult a resource to learn how to do a hanging indent on your word processing software.

Each style (MLA, APA, or other) has its own guidelines for formatting pages and other document elements. Below is a checklist for the basic formatting requirements for MLA and APA. This list is not exhaustive, and you may need to consult a resource to learn how to use your word processor to meet these guidelines.

MLA

• Margins are set to 1" on all four sides
• Heading in upper-left corner of first page only
• Heading includes: Writer Name, Title of Course, Name of Instructor, Date (Day #, month name in full, year)
• Title is centered and uses "Title Caps" (not bold, not underlined)
• Title appears on first page only
• All text in paper is exactly double-spaced
• Font is Times New Roman or similar
• Font size is set to 12pt
• Your last name and the page number are placed in the upper-right corner of each page
• Paragraphs are indented one tab
• No extra space between paragraphs

APA

• Includes APA style Title Page (see APA Style Guide)
• Margins are set to 1" on all four sides

- Running header includes title in upper-left corner on all pages
- Page numbers in upper-right corner on all pages
- All text in paper is exactly double-spaced
- Font is Times New Roman or similar
- Font size is set to 12pt
- Paragraphs are indented one tab
- No extra space between paragraphs

PRACTICE: Trade your paper with fellow students. Instead of reading for content, check the formatting of their in-text citations and "Works Cited," "References," or "Bibliography" page. Have they formatted their citations the same as you? If not, why not?

DRAFTING

After you have finished generating ideas and organizing your thoughts, you will want to begin your first draft. Here are some strategies to help you get started:

1. DON'T WORRY ABOUT BEING PERFECT

You don't have to worry about your draft being perfect the first time. Instead, try to write a complete, imperfect draft in one sitting without being concerned about perfect grammar or organization. Simply write out all of your ideas in full sentences and paragraphs. Remember, you can always revise later.

2. DRAFT FROM AN OUTLINE

An outline can help organize your ideas before you start writing a draft. (Students are often taught Roman numeral outlines, but writers outline in all sorts of formal or casual ways.) Once your outline is complete, begin your draft by writing a paragraph for each point. Stay flexible as you write and be ready to revise your organization or thesis if necessary.

3. DRAFT FROM A FREEWRITE

Revisit a freewrite or several related freewrites and underline the main points. Try to identify a main topic, a significant question that your topic raises, and the relevance of your topic. Then, begin your first draft with the strongest freewrite sentences that align well with your main topic.

4. TRUST YOUR THOUGHT PROCESS
If you have completed all of the techniques for generating ideas and you're still unsure where to begin, try to write a couple paragraphs reflecting on the ideas you've already generated. Since writing is a form of thinking, you may discover that you find a focus for your draft within the process of writing. Be open to those types of surprises—they might add depth and insight to your topic. If it doesn't work, you can always start again.

5. FAKE IT 'TIL YOU MAKE IT
Sometimes it's hard to know where to start, especially when you feel like you are not an expert on a subject. It may be difficult to speak with authority on a subject that you are just starting to understand. So, to begin, try faking it. Pretend you are an expert for a page or two, and see where it leads you.

6. PLAN TO WRITE MULTIPLE DRAFTS
You will likely have to compose several drafts in order to accomplish your assignment or goal. Try to plan time for revision, edits, and improvements.

PRACTICE: Spend twenty minutes using one of the above drafting strategies, then spend twenty minutes using another. Which strategy seemed most productive to you, and why? Did the different strategies produce different kinds of material? Which strategy will help produce a draft that most closely fits the requirements of the assignment?

EVALUATING SOURCES

Most of us are competent Internet searchers, good at finding movie times or what the weather will be like tomorrow. Researching for an academic paper is different, because you must evaluate the credibility, reliability, and accuracy of your sources. Online sources require particular scrutiny, because on the Internet, anyone can pretend to be an expert.

Below is a checklist to help you evaluate both text- and web-based sources.

AUTHORITY

- Are the author's qualifications (education or prior publications) listed?

- If there is more than one author, is there evidence that the content is accurate, knowledgeable, and/or unbiased about the subject?

- Is the publication reputable? Is a reference list or bibliography included?

DATE

> • Based on the date of publication, are the facts or opinions still timely? And, if it's a web source, is the last update noted?

INTENDED AUDIENCE

> • Is this publication intended for an academic, knowledgeable audience?

> • If the publication is intended for general readers, does this source satisfy the requirements of your assignment?

PURPOSE

> • If the publication takes a particular point of view, do you have other sources that cover other points of view?

SCOPE AND CONTENT

> • Is the subject matter covered relevant to your topic? Does it help clarify your ideas, or are you trying to "make it fit"?

PRACTICE: Complete the checklist on one or more of your sources. If the answer to most of the checklist questions is "no" or "I don't know," can you justify using the source?

EXPANDING IDEAS

So you've written your first draft and you're a couple pages short of the minimum page requirement. Some of the information needed to complete your essay might still be tucked away in your brain, or maybe you need to do more research to find further support for your ideas. The challenge is to find and develop new material that will strengthen your paper.

First, check your paper for instances of binary thinking: the belief that something is either good or bad, black or white. If you're asked to write about Gandhi, for instance, and you engage in binary thinking, then it's hard to write, because you think, "Well, Gandhi was good. Everyone knows that. What else is there to say?" A more complex consideration might describe Gandhi's beliefs and actions, interpret how he came to those beliefs, discuss why he took those actions, describe the effects of various events, explain how and why he changed over the years, and so forth. That way, you can write a much longer paper on Gandhi than you can if you interpret your topic as "Gandhi: Good or Bad?"

A second strategy is to play "devil's advocate." Read each of your paragraphs as a skeptic, finding every opportunity you can to ask *who?, what?, when?, where?, why?,* or *how?*. See if you can find a paradox, contradiction, or controversy related to your topic. For example:

> How much electricity—a major contributor to global warming—had to be used for the "Live Earth" concerts?

Write your questions in the margins or on a separate piece of paper, and then go back and answer them. Ask yourself where and how you can use examples to show the reader your points. Try to anticipate and address as many of the reader's questions as possible.

Another thing to check is that wherever you've quoted or paraphrased a source, you've also written something about that source. Think of your paper as a call-in radio show where you're the host: each time someone new is speaking, the host has to introduce who is talking and what makes him an expert, clarify what's just been said, and remind the person just tuning in what the discussion has been about. A strong paper introduces sources, interprets what they've said, and explains how those ideas relate to what you, the writer, have just said and are going to say next.

After you've expanded the ideas in your paper, you'll probably want to read it through again to see if your work has led to new insights about your topic. Good revision often helps you make a more complex central argument, which will need to be reflected in a different or more detailed thesis statement, and perhaps a revised conclusion. And by that point in your expansion work, it should be clear that your new material hasn't just made your paper longer, but also better.

PRACTICE: Look at your draft, or trade papers with a classmate. Ask at least one *who?, what?, when?, where?, why?,* or *how?* question for each paragraph in the draft. Rewrite the paragraphs to incorporate some answers to these questions.

FINDING SOURCES

Research takes time, and you'll also need time to order your thoughts on your assignment. As you begin to explore your topic, note what kinds of information you might need. Be sure to visit your library's web page and look for information and tutorials on using the library's catalogue, research databases, and web research tools. Even if you have used these resources in the past, brushing up and learning new ways of using them is always a good idea.

In order to familiarize yourself with the topic, you should begin with more general sources and overviews for background—encyclopedias, reviews, articles pertaining to your wider topic, and basic Internet searches are all great. Check your library web page again and look for a listing of all the databases you have access to, in the wide variety of subject areas.

Once you feel comfortable with your topic, the library is where you will find more specific sources to incorporate into your work—you have access to countless books, journals, and scholarly publications there. Think about whether what you find is current, relevant, biased, specific, or authoritative—all factors you will consider when evaluating your sources. (Review page 29 for help with evaluating your sources.) If the library doesn't have what you need, remember that you can often request materials from other libraries at no cost.

There are times, of course, that using the Internet makes sense. However, there's more to searching the Internet than typing terms into Google's standard home page. Below are some more effective strategies.

GOOGLE SCHOLAR (http://scholar.google.com/)

Google Scholar searches academic and peer-reviewed publications, while also pulling up similar pieces or touchstone works in the field. You may need to use the university's library to access full papers that Google Scholar offers only limited access to.

WIKIPEDIA (http://www.wikipedia.org/)

Most professors ask for more reliable and trustworthy sources than Wikipedia, because some Wikipedia articles appear to be written and researched by scholars, while others seem to be written with strong biases, limited knowledge, or by a public relations firm. However, Wikipedia entries should include reference lists, notes, and outside links—*those original sources* are the best places to start looking for more in-depth information.

If you're still stuck, more personalized help is available by visiting your library in person and asking a staff member there for help navigating the library's tools. You can even contact a subject librarian for assistance with research in specific subject areas. And consultants in your school's writing center can assist in getting your research on track at any point in your process of writing.

PRACTICE: Check out your library's research tools and tutorials. What resources are available that you haven't used or considered using before? Next, choose a topic and find a source from each of the resources listed above (i.e., Google Scholar, a reference librarian, etc.).

GENERATING IDEAS

LISTING

It's exactly what it sounds like. Every assignment, and every thesis, could go in many different directions. Before picking one direction, list as many as you can think of—write them down as fast as you can. Then, circle the interesting ones, which may be the basis for supporting ideas and paragraphs.

CLUSTERING

If you're a visual person and feel constricted writing paragraphs, try clustering. It's like free association. Write your main idea in the center of your paper and draw a circle around it. Now, quickly jot down ideas around your main idea, and any ideas that seem related to those—try to write related ideas together in the same area of the page, so that you end up with multiple "clusters" of thoughts or ideas on the page. Some clusters (you might circle the clusters, too) will probably end up with more material in them than others—these might indicate a central focus, a main argument, or just the primary topics your paper could cover.

CARDING

If you are a kinesthetic learner, try index cards. Write one idea
on a card, then a new idea on another card. Keep going until
you run out of ideas or cards. Go through your stack of cards
and write something new about each previous idea. See which
ideas change or develop. Spread out your cards and sort your
ideas into stacks. Some ideas may be related; others may be
irrelevant. If you are working on a research paper, this is also a
good way to sort through quotations you might use.

FREEWRITING

Start writing. Don't censor yourself. Keep your pen moving
no matter what comes out. Don't struggle to produce a perfect
sentence or worry about spelling or punctuation; just write
whatever pops into your head, even if it seems silly or off topic.
If you get stuck, write *I'm stuck*—or maybe something more
positive like *More thoughts soon*—as many times as you need
to, until a new thought occurs. (Writers often discover new
material after a few repetitions.) Try to write for five or ten
minutes. By freeing yourself up in this way you will be able to
get many of your ideas on paper, and afterward you can decide
which ones you would like to explore and expand.

LOOPING

After a five or ten minute freewrite, try to identify the most important or interesting sentence you've written, and circle or highlight it. Rewrite this sentence at the top of a new paragraph and freewrite again with this sentence as your starting point. This is a good way to explore your ideas in greater depth or detail without the pressure of more formal writing, and you can repeat the looping exercise as many times as feels useful.

PRACTICE: Before starting the first draft of your next essay, try one or more of these techniques for generating ideas: listing, clustering, carding, freewriting, or looping.

ORGANIZING AND OUTLINING

When beginning a paper, writers go through a process of generating thoughts and ideas regarding what they'll write about. After generating ideas, though, it's usually useful to organize them into a logical order or plan. The key to remember is that, as with a "working thesis," most first plans or outlines will need to change a bit as a piece of writing progresses.

Your essay might require a more complex structure than the following examples suggest, but these are general patterns you might consider for the organization of a draft:

- *General to Specific*: Start with a general statement, and then move toward more specific examples that support the general.

- *Specific to General*: Start with specific examples or details that serve to prove a larger, more general idea.

- *Chronological or Reverse Chronological*: Organize events in terms of when they happened—earliest to latest, or latest to earliest.

• If your essay is an argument, your argument might progress: claim, subclaim, support (evidence and examples), counterargument, rebuttal, definitions of problem, causes, effects, and solutions.

Below are some organizing or outlining methods you might try:

CLUSTERING

A great way to discover connections between your ideas quickly and visually, this method works similarly to the invention strategy on page 37. Jot down ideas as they come to you and watch for ways to draw them together.

IDEA TREE

With this top-down type of outline, you place a topic at the head of your page and begin "branching" off with supporting ideas and materials. You expand these "limbs" by branching off again with more details.

NESTING MODEL

The traditional, Roman numerals outline, this method involves putting main ideas in a I, II, III... order, with supporting material indented beneath in a i, ii, iii... list. You can keep adding more detailed claims as you go.

NOTECARDS

Put all of the topics and pieces of supporting evidence you wish to address on notecards, then spread them on the floor and arrange them.

PRACTICE: For your next essay, create an outline or guide using any of the strategies listed above. Which pattern of development makes the most sense, given the audience and goals of the essay? Try coming up with your own pattern of further development.

PARAGRAPHS

A paragraph is a collection of related sentences that explain, exemplify, or expand on a single idea. If a paragraph begins with an idea or major point of discussion (*raccoons steal my garbage*, for instance) it should not contain irrelevant facts (*Portland's curbside recycling system confuses me*), nor should it end with a different idea or point (*children's water guns can shoot over twenty feet*). A paragraph should just be about one thing. One. Freaking. Thing.

Well-constructed paragraphs usually contain the following:

TOPIC SENTENCE
A topic sentence is the paragraph's focus, idea, and/or thesis. The easiest way to make your idea clear is to put the topic sentence at the beginning of the paragraph.

ADEQUATE DEVELOPMENT
There is no set number of sentences that make a paragraph. However, the idea expressed in the topic sentence should be clear and supported by: discussing examples, details, facts, or statistics; using quotes and paraphrased material; examining

and evaluating causes and effects; and defining or describing terms.

COHERENCE

Coherence refers to a sense of logical connections. The idea in your topic sentence could develop further in each sentence. For example: "Mustard sandwiches are easy to make" could introduce a paragraph on how to make them.

Key words or ideas could appear throughout the paragraph. For example: A paragraph defining "conflict resolution" would naturally use one or both of those words in each sentence.

Use of parallel sentence structure in a paragraph can demonstrate connections. For example: "Paragraphs exploring a single idea can make a reader's job easier" and "Topic sentences stating a paragraph's focus can make a paper more coherent" both feature a [something] can [do something] structure.

Some reasons to begin a new paragraph include:
- To show you are switching to a new idea.
- To signal a change in time or place.
- To move to the next step in a process.
- To introduce a new source or alternate opinion.

Possible methods of ordering paragraphs in an essay include:

- Time (beginning to end, past to present, etc.)
- Space (moving through a location or scene)
- Rising tension (building toward a climax or conclusion)
- Importance (least to most important, or the reverse)

Just as a speaker who rambles for a long time without pausing soon becomes difficult to follow, if your whole paper was one long paragraph, your reader might get confused, give up, or just think you were insane. When each paragraph focuses on one thing, the content becomes easier for the audience to follow.

PRACTICE: Go through your paper and underline the topic sentence in each paragraph. Does the content of each paragraph match its topic sentence? If not, can you say what the paragraph is really about? If you have a hard time finding a topic sentence, how can you revise the paragraph so that it includes one?

PARAPHRASE, QUOTE, SUMMARIZE

Paraphrasing, quoting, and summarizing are three ways to bring sources into your writing. To understand their differences, take a look at the following passage about beef and three alternate ways to use it in a paper.

Original Passage: "A recent development in American nutrition is the move to buy and eat organic. Farming without pesticides has health benefits for both consumers and farmers, and environmental benefits as well—the choice to go organic is undoubtedly a good one. The trouble is 'organic' is not a guarantee of freshness, flavor, or nutrition. Nevertheless, the food industry has been quick to pick up on the organic trend and, as a result, the term 'organic' has come to mean less and less." —Ernest Bloom's "The Fruit Debacle"

Paraphrasing is restating a source's ideas in your own words. Paraphrased material tends to be roughly the same length as the passage being paraphrased, and does not use quotation marks. For example:

According to Bloom, many Americans enjoy eating produce,

and a large number have turned to organic sources. Farming organic foods used to imply farming that was free of chemicals and in which crops were treated with care, which not only made for healthier food, but also supported the health of the ecosystem and farm workers. Unfortunately, once big business realized how much interest was developing in "organic," the emphasis turned away from health and reverted back to making a profit (Bloom).

Quoting is using a source's exact words in your paper. A quote must be enclosed in quotation marks. It looks like this:

In a search for better health, many Americans have begun to eat organic. Unfortunately, "the food industry has been quick to pick up on the organic trend and, as a result, the term 'organic' has come to mean less and less" (Bloom).

Summarizing is condensing a source's main ideas into your own words. Summarized material is shorter than the passage being summarized and does not use quotation marks. Here's an example:

In his essay "The Fruit Debacle," Ernest Bloom approves of eaters who choose organic produce, but warns that use of the term "organic" within the industry doesn't always denote higher-quality taste.

It's important to know not only how paraphrasing, quoting, and summarizing are different, but also why you would want to use one technique instead of the other.

- Paraphrase a source when you want to simplify, clarify, or reorder a source's views to better suit its position or purpose in your paper. In general, rely most heavily on paraphrase. Your paper will "sound" more consistent when you put it in your own words, and the practice of translating your sources' ideas into your own paraphrases will help you better understand and analyze them.

- Quote a source when the exact words the author uses are distinctive in some way. Often this is because the original words are authoritative, precise, or powerful.

- Summarize a source when readers need to know the essential information, but not all of the details.

PRACTICE: Pick a passage from one of the essays in your textbook and practice paraphrasing, quoting, and summarizing it. Now, go through your paper draft with three different colored highlighters, one for each of the three tasks: paraphrase, quote, and summary. Once you've finished, look at your paper to see if one color dominates. Are you using the most effective technique in each situation?

PEER RESPONSE

Sharing your work can be an invaluable part of the writing process. Some students find it uncomfortable to offer feedback to others when they are still working on their own writing skills, but the process of looking at another writer's work as both a reader and a fellow writer can help improve our understanding of writing for the needs of the reader.

Before beginning a peer review, it's a good idea to ask the writer or your instructor for permission to mark on the work. Also, make sure that you're respectfully addressing the work itself rather than the writer. Your goal, and your peer's goal, is to improve the quality of the work not by criticizing the skills or abilities of the writer, but by informing the writer how a reader may respond to the piece. Below are some strategies for commenting on a peer's writing, with specific and helpful notes for avoiding common pitfalls.

Point to Specific Strengths

Often the most helpful comments are those that point to specific sentences, words, or images that stood out to the reader as memorable, understandable, or powerful. Discussing strengths doesn't mean adding a few bland compliments before attacking the work, but instead offering thoughtful reflections on what you found to be positive traits of the writing.

For example, look for moments where you as a reader find a point argued particularly well, where language is clearly communicating its meaning, or where there's strong use of an image. Regardless of the type of writing your peer is sharing, comments should be more than just "this is good." You should instead explain how a particular strength is working well. Why is it good? What about it strikes you when you're reading?

Problematic Moments for the Reader

Most drafts have moments that are weak, forgettable, or otherwise not working. A piece of writing may lose the reader when the writer's meaning becomes unclear or confusing and a part of the writing doesn't seem to fit within the larger context of the whole. Trouble spots in a work may happen at a syntax level (how words or sentences are arranged), an organizational level (order of paragraphs or ideas), a logical level (how the writer sees ideas connecting), or even a broader argument level (the argument itself may be problematic).

Again, good feedback not only points out where these moments occur ("this is bad" is a bad comment), but explains in greater detail why you, as a reader, had trouble there. (A good example would be "I found this confusing because you talk about 'perpetual motion' here, but don't explain the term until eight pages later.") While the ability to explain why the writing causes issues is valuable to your peer, it will also help you find these issues in your own writing.

Whether you're looking for strengths or weaknesses in the writing, the key factors to any good peer response are respectfully communicating to the writer where and how a reader may react, providing constructive feedback, and maintaining an open mind toward a peer's reading of your work. Ideally, both writers will walk away from the experience with a greater understanding of how a reader may interpret their words.

> **PRACTICE:** Have you ever considered marking one of your own drafts the way you might mark someone else's? Similarly, have you ever read a peer's writing and offered thoughts on it *without* making any marks on the paper? You might want to try both of these techniques if you haven't before.

PLACING SOURCES IN CONTEXT

When using sources in a research paper, it is not only important to choose your sources carefully, but also to introduce, interpret, and contextualize them. You can incorporate a source in your paper either by paraphrasing or by quoting directly. When using a quote in your essay, your own words should directly precede and follow the source, in order to show the quote's purpose and relevance to your argument. This is called framing a quote.

Consider the following example paragraph:

> Sometimes things aren't so easy. "The problem with their plan," psychologist Jane Smith said in an interview with Conrad Highwater on The American Mind, "is that they didn't account for the degrees to which people are controlled by forces that we can neither prove the existence of nor agree on the function of. I'm talking, of course, about the unconscious, or the subconscious, depending on whether you're Freudian or Jungian about things. And that actually makes a big difference, too, though that's not our first concern here."

This is a poorly framed quote—the writer hasn't contributed anything other than a brief introductory sentence, and it's unclear what kinds of "things" aren't so easy, or even what Smith is referring to. Moreover, the writer fails to provide any analysis, interpretation, or explanation after the quote. We, the readers, are left to guess about why the writer chose to include the quote and how it supports his or her own argument.

In the following paragraph, the writer introduces, interprets, and contextualizes the quote in a way that strengthens the essay:

> Dogs might salivate at the sound of a bell, but strict behavioral psychology fails to capture the more complex motivations behind human behavior. As psychologist Jane Smith notes in her interview with Conrad Highwater on The American Mind, early behaviorists "didn't account for the degrees to which people are controlled by forces that we can neither prove the existence of nor agree on the function of." As Smith indicates, regardless of whether one ascribes to Freudian, Jungian, or some other psychology, most people have experienced moments in which forces deeper than the sound of a bell seemed to be pushing them to choose one action over another.

In the first example, an unfocused quote dominated the paragraph, with no explanation or contextualization from the writer. In the second example, the quote was trimmed to its most useful point and placed within a context the writer controlled. To make better use of the quote, the writer has chosen to paraphrase some of Smith's argument, rather than quoting all of it. In the second example, it is much clearer how we are meant to understand the quote within the context of the essay.

It is also important to use appropriate verbs when introducing your quotes. Some writers will use verbs such as "says" or "argues" repeatedly throughout their paper. These verbs are not incorrect. However, choosing more specific verbs can clarify your intentions and enhance the strength of your argument. Verbs such as "believes" or "reports" differentiate between opinion and fact. If you wanted to emphasize the controversial nature of the discussion, you might use verbs like "contends" or "insists." Consult the chart on the following page when selecting verbs for introducing evidence.

Purpose	Verbs
Stating Facts	• reports that • states that • says that • points out that • mentions that • verifies that
Stating Opinions	• asserts that • claims that • argues that • believes that • maintains that • thinks that
Questioning	• denies that • contends that • complains that • rejects that • refutes that

PRACTICE: Choose an idea (quote, paraphrase, graph, stat, etc.) from a source that you want to integrate into your essay. Write an introduction before, and a response after, the source material, so that you interpret and contextualize the material and tie it to a main idea in your essay. Compare your paragraph with paragraphs written by other students, or with paragraphs in another text that uses outside sources.

PROOFREADING LOG

A proofreading log helps you keep track of errors you make in your writing, learn how to fix those errors, and, ultimately, avoid making those mistakes in the future. It's a tool for teaching yourself to correct your own papers. Here's one example:

Mistake	Rule	How I'll remember it	Correction
"*Its'* all good."	*It's* = it is	The apostrophe looks like the dot of an i.	"*It's* all good."

Would someone really remember that *it's* = *it is* by thinking that the apostrophe in between the *t* and the *s* of *it's* looks like the top of the *i* that has been taken out? Well, we do, and that's one of the attractions of the editing log: You can use your own best system for learning and remembering stuff—it's like a textbook written for you, by you. The examples come straight from your own papers, so you don't have to read a bunch of stuff that doesn't really apply to you.

If you use the same handbook or grammar guide all the time, you might even write the important page numbers down.

Here's an example:

Mistake	Rule	Page # in handbook	Correction
"There ain't no hope."	Professors hate ain't.	p. 153 "common errors"	"There is no hope."

You can set up your proofreading log however you want, but some of our suggestions are:

- Keep it nearby. We made ours with blue graph paper, then glued it to the back of our notebook.

- Keep it for a term. By the end of fall term, we had five or six entries, which meant five or six mistakes we weren't making any more.

- Show it to your professor when you ask to revise your paper for a better grade. He or she might—just might—be impressed. (It's worth a shot.)

PRACTICE: Take the last paper that you got instructor comments on. Create new entries in your proofreading log based on your instructor's comments (even the positive ones). Now, you've got a head start.

PROOFREADING STRATEGIES

Proofreading—finding and fixing errors in spelling, grammar, and punctuation—is really the last step in writing something. It's analogous to that last look in the mirror to check for scary hair or stuff in your teeth: you wouldn't want to check before you showered and brushed, but you wouldn't want to skip it, either. It's the small details that make your appearance and your writing seem polished.

When we read our own work, our eye often runs ahead, causing us to miss some mistakes, especially if we're reading on a computer screen. The key to catching errors is to s l o w d o w n. Read your draft sentence by sentence backwards, or read line-by-line using a ruler or piece of paper to cover the rest of the text as you go.

Another way to catch errors is to listen. Read your piece out loud. Better yet, have someone else read it out loud to you exactly as you've written it—typos and all. You'll be able to hear awkward sentence constructions, redundancies, and odd transitions.

Maybe you have some old papers lying around with marks your professor made. Look at your misspelled words or any comments about your sentences, and make a list of errors you might search for in your current paper. (For more about this, see "Proofreading Log" on p. 57.)

Use your computer's spell check, but don't rely on it completely. Their are dimes when they won't catch errors because the wrong word is spilt write.

PRACTICE: First, find four errors in the paragraph above. Next, go through your own paper as slowly as possible, with a pen in hand. Make a tally at the top of the page for every error you find and correct. When you've finished, look at your tally and congratulate yourself. Each of those errors might have been marked by the teacher. You may have just improved your grade!

RESEARCH

Most students expect that the process of writing a research paper looks something like this:

1. Figure out what you're going to say in your paper.

2. Find the number of sources you're required to have, and make sure they match what you want to say.

3. Read and take notes from the sources.

4. Write the paper, plugging in notes from the research.

5. Receive a B or better.

While this process *may* work for some, it rarely leads to the kind of in-depth, carefully rendered analysis most instructors are looking for in a researched essay.

Like writing, researching is recursive, or repetitive in nature. In the same way your first thesis statement is a "working thesis," the research you do on your first forays into cyberspace and the library will be your "working knowledge." You likely won't find The Five Best Sources In the Universe on your first (or even second) search for information, so just as your working thesis statement will evolve as you research and write, so will your source material need to change in order to support, refine, or expand your new and improved thesis statement. In other words, while writing, you will probably need to re-search (get it?) for new sources in order to support your ideas.

A good process might look like this:

> 1. Come up with a decent idea, one that will likely still be interesting to you after several visits to the library and a dozen cybersearches.

> 2. Come up with a list of questions you want or need to answer in order to pursue your ideas.

> 3. Do some researching, note-taking, and daydreaming to find answers to your questions or to open up problematic counter-questions.

> 4. Write a draft.

5. In the afterglow of your attentively-written draft, figure out what you're really trying to say. What are the questions now? How have your questions changed, or have they stayed the same?

6. Do more research. Look in places you didn't look before (e.g., ask a reference librarian for help, find an expert to interview, etc.).

7. Write another draft.

8. Repeat steps 3-7 as necessary.

9. Finish excellent paper.

PRACTICE: Before you write, come up with a topic and write a list of twenty questions you have about it. If you're stumped, try the standard journalistic questions: *who? what? why? where? when? how?* From your twenty questions, pick five to research. Then, after you write, use the devil's advocate activity on page 31 to develop a new list of research questions. Pick the most important five questions, and do more research in order to find the answers.

REVISING FOR FLOW

Almost every writer hopes his or her project will have that magical, elusive quality called "flow." A good first draft, however, is often the result of searching for connections, and that search might naturally involve repetitions, false starts, or daring leaps—in other words, moments of chaos. A desire for "flow," then, is usually a way of saying you want to better organize your paper. An well-organized paper typically consists of paragraphs that transition logically and relate directly to your main point or thesis.

During the process of writing and revising, you may stray from the original structure or outline. Try to remain flexible in this process, reconsidering the organization when appropriate. When revising, the following questions or techniques may improve your focus and organization.

QUESTIONS TO ASK

What does this have to do with my thesis?
Sometimes, if you are passionate about a particular topic, you might digress from your original argument. During these

moments you can make a choice: either cut content unrelated to your thesis, or follow the digression and write a new thesis statement. Digressions can be a nightmare, but can also be a thrilling journey into a more nuanced approach to your subject, depending on your disposition. In either case, the key to a well-organized academic essay is a clear thesis, without distracting fluff.

Haven't I said this already?

Repetition often happens in the first draft. As we search for the best methods to support our thesis, we might use the same evidence more than once, restate conclusions, or redefine terms while attempting to clarify our meanings. By the time we start a second draft, though, we should have a better idea of where to keep important information, and how to remove anything we've needlessly repeated.

Are the transitions logical?

Sometimes paragraphs and sentences can seem disconnected or fragmented in an early draft. Transitions help correct this problem by logically connecting sentences, paragraphs, and sections in your paper; they are the connective tissue that binds ideas together. Transitions also give readers important cues that show how your thoughts relate to your argument.

TECHNIQUES

Reverse Outline

A reverse outline helps you identify structural weaknesses and evaluate whether or not your structure is working. There are several approaches to this process.

Try writing a one-sentence summary of each paragraph and its purpose within your paper (i.e. how the paragraph proves your thesis). Paragraphs commonly: introduce, describe, propose, list, question, define, and conclude. If you notice, for example, that a paragraph defines the parameters of your argument, but it comes after a paragraph that proposes a solution, you might consider rearranging those paragraphs so that when you propose a solution, your reader can understand your progression.

Another reverse outline technique is to highlight your thesis and topic sentences for each paragraph. Then, on a separate piece of paper, write out the thesis and topic sentences in the order they appear. In doing this, you create a new outline for your project, and you may also discover where your new outline does not progress logically. In this case, you have an opportunity to revise the structure, rearranging the paragraphs accordingly. Likewise, difficulty locating your thesis or topic sentences can indicate that you need to rewrite them. Remember, each topic sentence should tell us something about the paragraph's contents and how that content supports your thesis.

Writing Transitions

For readers to follow your train of thought, you must show how two ideas connect and signal what kind of transitions you are making. Sometimes a paragraph will require an entire transitional sentence. Other times, you can use a transitional word or phrase that guides readers to where your text is headed. Specifically, transitions tell readers whether you're restating a point ("in other words"), adding something ("additionally"), offering an example ("for example"), showing an effect ("as a result"), or qualifying a claim ("and yet"). To work on transitions, look at your paragraphs and write a sentence, word, or phrase that connects them. (Hint: Transitions usually work best in the first sentence of a new paragraph, but they can sometimes be effective when placed in the last sentence of the preceding paragraph.)

Cut and Paste

Finally, there's old-fashioned cutting and pasting with scissors and tape. It can be quite gratifying to cut up an essay by hand and rearrange paragraphs on the floor, especially if you've been dying to tear the thing up and throw it away. Scrutinize each paragraph next to the thesis. Does it support, define, or explain your thesis? If not, trash it. When you're done and have a pile of quality paragraphs, you can shuffle them until the order seems right. Then, tape them together on new paper with spaces between for notes. Those notes might say things like, "transition?" or "need new paragraph here to define terms." The cut and paste technique may sound silly at first, but it's a good way to physically reorganize your paper, see what maintains your main focus, and identify what material is tangential or unrelated.

> **PRACTICE**: The paragraphs you just read explain how to decide whether your paper is nicely organized or not. Try printing out an extra copy of your double-spaced draft, then cutting it up and rearranging it as described above. Throw in a few blank slips of paper in case you need to add transitions, and then tape it all back together.

REVISING FOR STYLE

WORDINESS

Do you feel like you don't have enough to say? Well, the solution is to offer more thoughts, not more words. (To generate more thoughts, revisit pages 31-33.) Words without thoughts are confusing, and readers often find them pretentious or obnoxious. For example:

> After much consideration, I have come to the opinion that the character of Holden Caulfield, the main character in the novel *The Catcher in the Rye*, is definitely seen as being a character that is in possession of very many numerous flaws. These flaws are large in size, and because of the fact that these flaws make it very incredibly hard for Holden Caulfield to have honest relationships, the character of Holden Caulfield, in my opinion, really needs professional psychological help to help with his mental state.

That sounds pretty obnoxious, and what's worse, it doesn't say much. Let's try eliminating some of the unnecessary words.

Here are some tricks to try:

1. Eliminate references to the 1st person.
   For example: "After much consideration, I have come to the opinion that..." Or, "In my opinion..."

2. Eliminate unnecessary adverbs and intensifiers.
   For example: "definitely," "very," and "incredibly."

3. Eliminate repeated nouns—especially full names.
   For example: Use pronouns ("he," "him," "them," "it") or just last names instead.

4. Eliminate "a character."
   For example: Change "Holden Caulfield" to "him," or simply "Caulfield."

5. Simplify. If it's obvious or unnecessary, eliminate it.
   For example: Change "large in size" to "large," and "that is in possession of" to "that has."

6. Make passive verbs active— wherever it's not clear who is doing the action.
   For example: Change "is seen as being" to "is."

Now, here's how it reads:

> Holden Caulfield, the main character in *The Catcher in the Rye*, has numerous flaws, and because they make it hard for him to have honest relationships, he needs professional psychological help.

It's still not perfect, but at least it's clear and accurate.

PARALLELISM

Readers often find it easier (and more pleasant) when the grammatical structures of a sentence gracefully match up. In the world of words we call it "parallelism." Without it, sentences can feel chaotic. Think about a PowerPoint slide. What if you saw this list in PowerPoint?

> We need to: —fire John
>   —hire Matt.
>   —mailing list.

Which one of these things doesn't belong? "Mailing list" is the only one that doesn't start with an action, and it's also the only one that doesn't work with the introduction. That's the difference between parallel lists and nonparallel lists: *parallel lists match up*. Be parallel by checking tense, number, and whether the list parts all match up with the sentence opening. (For famous examples of the use of parallel structures, check out Dr. Martin Luther King, Jr.)

SENTENCE VARIETY

Think of how boring life would be if every song on the radio followed the same chord progression, or every TV show had the same story line. In writing, as in life, we have the power to rearrange the parts, spice up our narratives, and inject variety into otherwise boring patterns. (Did you notice the cool parallelism in that sentence? It was:

> We have the power to: —rearrange the parts.
> —spice up our narratives.
> —inject variety.)

When thinking about variety, consider this example:

> "Holden Caulfield has a difficult time obeying the law. He also has a difficult time with religion. He thinks social networks are like a game. He doesn't play the game well."

First, vary the length of your sentences. Think rhythm—count the number of beats in each sentence; variation makes a paragraph easier to read, because novelty creates excitement. Second, vary the openings of your sentences. The pronoun "he" begins nearly every sentence in the above example. Mix it up a little.

Consider this revision:

> Holden Caulfield has a difficult time with law and religion. He thinks social networks are a game, and because he doesn't play this game very well, he goes a little crazy at the end.

PRACTICE: Choose a paragraph from your writing. See how many words you can cut before the meaning gets lost. How do the two versions compare? Tip—Look for the following words: *that, which, it, there, as, is, was, are, were, of*. These words often occur in wordy phrases.

REVISING FROM COMMENTS

IDEAS

Revising in response to instructor or peer feedback requires a good deal of critical thinking, and should comprise the bulk of your revision time (see p. 31 for hints on expanding ideas). Look for notes, comments, or questions like these:

IDEAS

• *Clarify*: A commenter who writes this is not understanding your idea or point. It might be useful here to look over this section and try, in a simple sentence, to articulate what your point actually is. How can you make this easier to understand for your reader? Maybe it's a matter of defining key terms, explaining cause and effect, connecting ideas to your larger thesis, or just finding a simpler way to say what you intended.

• *How? / Why? / So What?*: These types of comments can mean a couple of things. Similar to the "Clarify" comment, these questions may indicate that your reader does not understand your specific argument or claim. Why are you writing what you are writing in this section, and how does it relate to the central idea of your piece? Connecting your ideas to a larger point or argument (thesis) is crucial for strong academic writing. This does not mean that your paper must take on global issues and seasoned experts—though it can. It simply means that your writing should engage in a larger conversation about the topic.

• *Expand / Explore / Elaborate / Develop*: These phrases are used for a number of reasons. Perhaps your main idea needs more detail, or maybe the reader thinks a particular point is especially strong and wants more. In either case, you need to say more in order to refine your argument.

• *Support / Explain*: Evidence is central to any good assertion. What type of evidence you use depends on what type of paper you are writing.

• *Transition*: This means that the connection between two paragraphs or sections of your essay is not clear. You may need to write a few sentences to make the connection clear, or you may need to rearrange paragraphs so that one idea leads smoothly to the next in your paper. (For more on this, consult "Revising for Flow" on p. 64.)

• *Reword / Rephrase*: This comment is asking you to think of another way to present an idea. Perhaps it is unclear as is, or perhaps you have reused the same key terms or phrases too often. Saying your ideas multiple ways can be challenging, but also offers the opportunity to strengthen your claim by being more specific.

(RE)ORGANIZATION

¶: Readers make this symbol when they feel you've switched to a new topic that deserves its own, fully-developed paragraph.

Arrows / Lines / Movement: Your reader might highlight sections of text and suggest that those sections be rearranged for a number of reasons. Often a suggestion that you move a section of the paper requires more than just copying and pasting, but reworking the text so that it fits in with another section of the paper. For example, if your reader suggests that one section might be stronger in the introduction, you may need to take the ideas and thoughts from that section and work them into the introduction, rather than simply moving the entire section into your already formed introduction.

GRAMMAR

These comments refer to those annoying little problems that need to be fixed in the final phase of revision to produce a polished essay. Check any style guide for a more complete list of common symbols.

- *Awk*: Awkward, typically because the sentence is worded unusually, and should be simpler or more precise.

- *Cliché*: Clichés are overused language. Think "playing with fire" or "like a bull in a china shop." Instead of relying on a cliché, use your own words and imagery.

- *CS*: Comma splice, or two sentences that have been joined incorrectly by a comma. Break these into two sentences with a period or semicolon, or join them with a connecting word like "and" or "but."

• *Frag*: Sentence fragment—a way of saying the sentence is incomplete. If there is no subject, verb, or independent clause of any kind, you have not made a sentence.

• *Run-on*: Two or more independent clauses stuck together without punctuation. Try breaking clauses up into smaller sentences or using connecting words (e.g., "because," "and," "but") to show relationships.

•*Sp*: The word is misspelled.

PRACTICE: Before you revise, read through your peer review notes and instructor's comments, making a list of feedback. Use your list to write a revision strategy—a plan for which issues you'll address and how you'll address them in your next draft.

REVISING THESIS STATEMENTS

It's normal for your first attempts at making a debatable claim to be a bit rough. A thesis statement that might need some more work can often be one that:

- Makes no debatable claim, such as: *This paper will examine the pros and cons of death.*

- Is obvious, or a statement of fact, such as: *Death is very scary to some people.*

- Offers personal belief or folk wisdom as its claim, such as: *A positive attitude will help you succeed.*

- Makes an overly broad claim, such as: *Sex sells.*

If you suspect your thesis could be stronger or more focused, think about playing bad cop and bringing it in to the station downtown for questioning. Grilling your thesis can be done before you start your first draft or when revising a later draft—anytime you want to make sure the thesis is saying something that makes for a useful argument and is what you really mean.

To start this process, first ask questions that rule out the above weaknesses. Then try asking the thesis *who? what? when? where? why?* or *how?* questions that seek clarification. For example:

THESIS: The media is very influential in today's society.

YOU: That's an obvious statement or fact—shouldn't you be debatable, Thesis? Is there even an opposing viewpoint to that?

THESIS: Uh, the media is not very influential in today's society?

YOU: That's ridiculous. No one would argue that. You're wasting my time here. What do you mean by "society"? By "the media"?

THESIS: Teenagers are greatly influenced by television programming.

YOU: How are they influenced? Where? When? This will all go easier if you just tell me.

THESIS: Okay, okay, um: Modern American teens are greatly influenced in their dress, language, and attitudes by television programming.

YOU: Why? WHY?!

THESIS: I don't know, man. Maybe it's, maybe it's, maybe it's because American teens are particularly peer conscious and therefore are more likely to be influenced by advertising during television programming than other demographics.

YOU: Okay. Now we're getting somewhere.

At a certain point, you'll want to really give your thesis a hard time and ask it questions like: "Oh yeah, well what about...?" And, of course, the classic: "So what?" Then your thesis really starts to shape up.

THESIS: Despite the prevalent iconography of the rebellious adolescent, American teens are increasingly influenced by television advertising and are becoming more culturally homogenous than ever before.

A strong thesis statement can incorporate and embrace contradictions or opposing viewpoints. (That's why thesis statements often include the words "however" or "although.") If in the course of reading, researching, or writing, you encounter conflicting evidence or interpretations, don't immediately abandon your thesis. Take advantage of those complications to expand, qualify, and refine your thesis until you find the most accurate explanation of the evidence you can manage.

When you've finished this interrogation, you'll also have a useful byproduct: a list of questions you can use to make sure you've got good definitions, evidence, and source material to back up your assertions.

PRACTICE: Using the model of the thesis interrogation in this chapter, ask *who? what? when? where? why? how?* and *so what?* questions of your thesis (or, you also can use a classmate's). Then rewrite your thesis so that it addresses the questions, and, using the list at the beginning of this chapter, test your thesis.

USING SOURCES TO REVISE

Imagine you just began research for a paper. You believe that the media is solely to blame for women becoming obsessed with unhealthy and unobtainable beauty ideals, and will write about that. You skim the first four articles you find and are pleased that all of them agree that the media *is* responsible for women's obsessions with being rail-thin, tan, and Barbie-doll-shaped. "Wonderful!" you exclaim, "I'll now be able to use all four of these sources to support my argument!"

After you use your sources to support your thesis in the first pages of your draft, though, you begin to get the feeling that your writing isn't saying anything new. You're just repeating your sources, so you decide to do a little more research.

Returning to the databases—or after consulting with a reference librarian—you find several more articles that agree that the media is to blame, and one article titled, "Americans Need to Take Responsibility For Their Viewing Habits." Intrigued, you skim through it. You are shocked to learn that the author believes that not only women, but men, as well, are *themselves* responsible for how they let the media influence their conceptions of beauty and self-image.

Suddenly, a world of complications opens up. Because you decided to do more research, you found an article that makes your topic more interesting. But you also feel uneasy—after reading this article, you no longer feel sure that your point (to prove that the media is to blame) is correct. What now?

Bravely, you start freewriting about your new complications:

> OK, first I thought my thesis was that the media was totally to blame; then I found this weird article that made me think twice—are people to blame for the way they are influenced by the media's ideals about what is and isn't attractive? This makes sense, but I don't think it is <u>completely</u> up to people either; before people can take responsibility for their ideals about beauty, they have to become <u>aware</u> of the influence media has on them!

You now feel like you have an original idea. You revise your thesis statement to read, "The media greatly influences what men and women believe to be attractive. However, men and women also have a choice as to whether and how often they expose themselves to what the media offers. American society should work toward awareness of the influence that the media has over them, so that people can better control that influence."

You now have a thesis statement that isn't simply repeating one of your sources. Your new thesis uses many (even opposing) elements from each source, which adds originality and complexity. Feeling brilliant, you move forward with your new thesis.

PRACTICE: Find a source that has a different point of view from an assertion you make in your draft. Freewrite about the discrepancy, and see if you can come up with a new assertion, argument, or thesis that accounts for the discrepancy.

WRITING ABOUT PERSONAL EXPERIENCE

Though some students may be more comfortable than others about sharing personal experiences, being asked to write about yourself is common in undergraduate courses. Describing your experiences in effective ways will help you craft your writing into clear and compelling narratives.

Before you begin writing about your own experience, ask yourself two important questions: "Who will read this essay?" and "What is the intended purpose of this essay?" If you're applying to dental school and the school of your dreams requires a personal statement about why you'd like to be a dentist, you might start by brainstorming a list of all of the personal experiences in your life—the first time you brushed your teeth, the six years you spent shadowing a dentist, the time you chipped your tooth and a dentist fixed it for you, etc.—that relate to dentistry and your budding interest in the subject. From there, hone the list into a cluster of related moments that take the reader of your application on a journey, from the time you first chipped your tooth and had it fixed, to the years you spent shadowing doctors, to applying to dental school, and even as you see yourself in the future.

It may seem simple enough to choose a topic for something like dental school, but what if your teacher assigns a personal essay and allows you to choose from any personal experience? There are a variety of strategies for sifting through the large number of memories and encounters you've accumulated throughout your life. You might brainstorm about moments in which you've changed in some way, freewrite about people or places that are significant to you, or even just flip through photographs looking for unexpected moments that seem connected.

In a traditional personal essay, you don't necessarily have to make an argument—the essay can simply illustrate a moment of self-discovery, reflect on a difficult time, or contain a series of moments strung together to complete a narrative. The goal of writing personal experiences is not to list as many facts or memories about yourself as you can, but to construct a meaningful piece of writing from incidents about which you are an authority, since you lived them.

Of course any moment can be made significant, whether you are writing about a car crash or a car trip, a first job or a third. The importance lies not within the moment(s) you choose to describe, but in how you choose to tell them. Keep in mind who you are writing for and what the purpose of the writing is. Remove details that seem irrelevant or distracting. For example, in your dental school personal statement, it may be unnecessary to tell the reader that you once taught preschool kids how to recycle or that you enjoy playing volleyball on the weekends. Similarly, if you're writing a personal essay about a trip you took with your family, it might not be necessary to describe each photo that you took with your family while there. Keep the details in these essays relevant and ask yourself what work each detail is doing. If a detail isn't relating back to and supporting the main point of your essay, the reader will be better off without it.

PRACTICE: Freewrite for five or ten minutes about a personal experience, or about a person you know closely. Next, look for a theme or some kind of connection in the observations you've written, and revise your freewrite by adding thoughts about material that relates to the theme. (This could also involve another freewrite.) Finally, trim details that may be irrelevant or unnecessary. Your result may be something that could be the beginning or focus of a larger essay.

WRITING THESIS STATEMENTS

The thesis statement goes by many names: *central point,*
assertion, or *argument,* to name a few. Often one or two
sentences long, a thesis statement usually appears near the
beginning of an essay—many college teachers expect that it will
appear at the end of your first paragraph. It usually consists
of two parts: the *topic* and the *assertion or argument* you will
make about the topic in your paper. For example:

> "Although often portrayed as the quintessential vampire
> in literature and movies, Dracula [topic] was not the first,
> nor the most significant vampire [assertion]."

Your thesis needs to be debatable, a position that can be
supported or proven with logic and evidence. Don't let the
thought of having to "prove" something fluster you, though—
you just need to make a solid case.

Some ways to get started include:

> • Write a list of questions you might ask about your topic,
> and circle the one that you care most about that fits the

assignment. Next, write a list of more questions related to that question. Looking at those questions, create a theory that *answers* one or more of them. That theory, as crazy as it sounds, might be your thesis.

• Look for a paradox, contradiction, or problem related to your topic. Write your thesis so that it points out this complication.

• You might try fitting your information into a structure like this: "Although at first it seems _____, upon closer inspection it is clear that _____."

Sometimes you don't really know what you're writing about—or your thoughts and feelings on it—until you've written a few pages. Learning about something by writing about it is normal, so there's no reason to worry if your original thesis statement seems imperfect or less accurate as you write more of your paper. That original thesis statement has simply turned out to be a "working thesis" that has helped you charge ahead and get a draft written.

If by the end of the paper your working thesis doesn't turn out to be what you feel anymore, that's fine. For most writers, trying to carefully produce five "perfect" pages in one draft is far more painful than writing a draft with a working thesis, and then going back to revise.

Revising your working thesis into a stronger statement will probably also require you to do some revision within the body of your first draft, as well. Those kind of changes are good—they indicate that you're narrowing in on exactly what you're arguing, and you're adjusting your paper to prove that argument. The important thing is that you shouldn't be married to your first thoughts on a topic—you "work on" your paper as you write it. That's why it's called a working thesis.

PRACTICE: Write the opposite of your thesis. If that's difficult, is your current thesis too general? Then write three versions of your working thesis. Try at least one using one of the following words: *although, however, because,* or *despite.* Share your three versions with your peers and ask them to test each one: 1) Does your thesis include a topic and an assertion about the topic; 2) Is it debatable, and; 3) Does it promise to explore or explain a paradox, a contradiction, or a problem?

WORKS CITED

Bloom, Ernest. "The Fruit Debacle." *Fruit Farm Weekly*. May
2009.

Smith, Jane. Interview with Conrad Highwater. *The American
Mind*. Natl. Public Radio. WFAK, Springfield. 10, Jun.
2008.